ANNIE'S ATTIC
CROCHET

TABLE OF CONTENTS

MEET THE DESIGNER

Trish Hoskin is a celebrated crochet designer, author a coach with over 25 years of experience in the craft imaginative and expertly designed patterns, Tri dedicated following through Fat Lady Croche nostalgic and innovative crochet designs that bring joy to makers of all skill levels.

With a passion for storytelling through stitches, Trish's work blends creativity with technical precision, making her patterns both fun to create and visually striking. Her designs have been featured in top crochet magazines. When she's not designing playful, personality-filled crochet pieces, Trish can often be found on wheels—whether practicing roller disco or channeling her derby spirit. Her creativity and passion for movement fuel her work, inspiring crocheters to bring a little fun and flair into every stitch.

BASIC CUBIE BODY

Here you will find a step-by-step tutorial for creating the nice squared off look of the cubie body that is shared in each of the animals in this book.

SKILL LEVEL

Confident Beginner

FINISHED MEASUREMENT

Body is 5 inches square

MATERIALS

- Premier Yarns Anti-Pilling Everyday Worsted medium (worsted) weight acrylic yarn (3½ oz/180 yds/ 100g per skein):
  1 skein #100-81 porcelain blue
- Size G/6/4mm crochet hook
- Tapestry needle
- Polyester fiberfill

GAUGE

9 sc = 2 inches; 9 rows = 2 inches

Exact gauge is not critical for this project.

PATTERN NOTES

The photos shown here are for illustration only. They show fewer stitches in each row and fewer rows in each Square. Make sure to follow the written instructions.

Weave in loose ends as work progresses unless otherwise stated.

The cubes are worked in 6 separate Squares and sewn together. The Squares are worked in rows.

Stuff firmly, but not so the stuffing shows through the stitches.

For Cubies with Striped or Color-Blocked Squares, follow the order of joining given in the individual pattern.

BASIC CUBE BODY

SQUARE

Make 6.

Row 1: Ch 19, sc in 2nd ch from hook and each rem ch across, turn. *(18 sc)*

Rows 2–18: Ch 1, sc in first and each st across, turn.

Fasten off, leaving a long tail for sewing.

ASSEMBLY

Once all Squares for Cube Body have been made, whipstitch them tog to create body cube, following instructions that follow.

Scan the code for a complete video how-to bonus project: the Beginner Cubie Cat.

Take **any 2 Squares** *(see Pattern Notes)* and match them along 1 side with long tail of 1 Square in top right corner for sewing. Whipstitch through edges of both Squares at same time, working whipstitches evenly across side. Whipstitches will be on outside of body. Run yarn tail under several sts on inside of body to secure. You do not need to trim yarn tail, but you may.

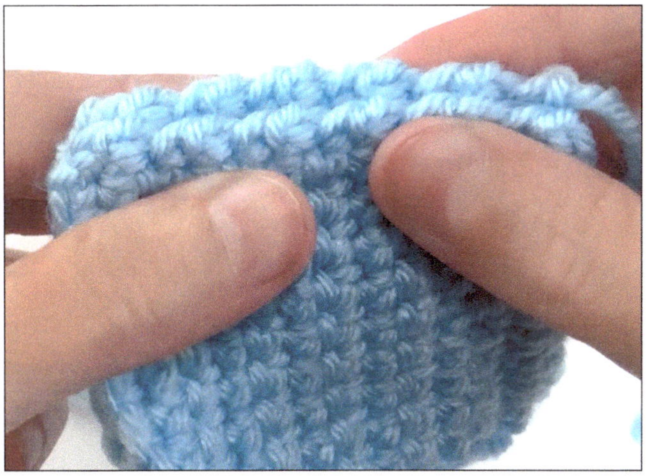

Create a line of squares by taking the next Square and aligning it along the side of 1 of 2 Squares just sewn tog, again with yarn tail in place to use it to whipstitch pieces tog. Continue with 1 more Square to have 4 Squares joined along sides.

Whipstitch rem side of 4th Square to open side of first Square to create box shape.

Take another Square and place it on top of box. Whipstitch this Square in place around all sides.

Rotate cube to sew final Square to bottom. Whipstitch around 3 sides, but don't secure yarn tail yet. **Stuff** *(see Pattern Notes)* with fiberfill until firm but not bulging. Fiberfill will squish down over time so be sure you have cube firmly filled. Once stuffed, whipstitch final side closed. Set aside. ●

TOM SMILING TIGER

Embrace the exotic by creating this little cubed tiger or play with the color combos for a more domesticated version of this fun design.

SKILL LEVEL

Confident Beginner

FINISHED MEASUREMENT

Body is 5 inches square

MATERIALS

- Premier Yarns Anti-Pilling Everyday Worsted medium (worsted) weight acrylic yarn (3½ oz/180 yds/ 100g per skein):
  - 1 skein each #100-01 snow white, #100-12 black and #100-94 pumpkin
- Size G/6/4mm crochet hook or size needed to obtain gauge
- Tapestry needle
- Stitch marker
- Polyester fiberfill
- ½-inch black buttons: 2*

**For use by children under 3 years of age, embroider eyes with black yarn.*

GAUGE

9 sc = 2 inches; 9 rows = 2 inches

Exact gauge is not critical for this project.

PATTERN NOTES

Each cubie is created by making 6 separate Squares flat and then sewing them together using whipstitches. Remaining pieces are worked separately and sewn on.

Leave a long tail for sewing on each remaining piece as specified. Weave in all other loose ends as work progresses unless otherwise stated.

Work remaining pieces in continuous rounds; do not join or turn unless otherwise stated. Place stitch marker at beginning of round and move up as each round is completed.

When changing color on Striped Squares, Legs and Tail, carry unused color loosely up until next needed if not instructed to fasten off.

Join with a slip stitch unless otherwise stated.

Stuff firmly, but not so the stuffing shows through the stitches.

SPECIAL STITCH

Single crochet color change (sc color change): Insert hook in indicated st, yo, pull up a lp *(2 lps on hook)*, drop current color, yo with new color, draw through both lps *(see illustration)*.

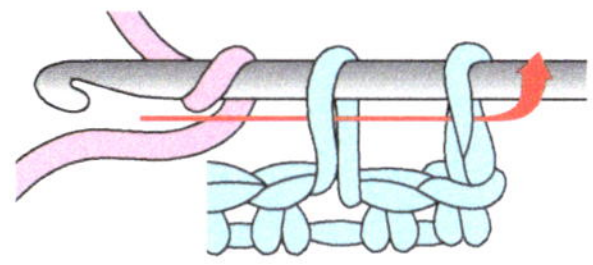

Single Crochet Color Change

TIGER

BASIC CUBE BODY

SOLID SQUARE

Make 3 with pumpkin.

See Basic Cube Body Square on page 2.

STRIPED SQUARE

Make 3.

Row 1: With pumpkin, ch 19, sc in 2nd ch from hook and each rem ch across, turn. *(18 sc)*

Rows 2–4: Ch 1, sc in first and each st across, turn. In last st of row 4, **sc color change** *(see Special Stitch and Pattern Notes)* to black. *(18 sc)*

Rows 5 & 6: Ch 1, sc in first and each st across, turn. In last st of row 6, sc color change to pumpkin. *(18 sc)*

Rows 7 & 8: Ch 1, sc in first and each st across, turn. In last st of row 8, sc color change to black. *(18 sc)*

Rows 9 & 10: Ch 1, sc in first and each st across, turn. In last st of row 10, sc color change to pumpkin. *(18 sc)*

Rows 11 & 12: Ch 1, sc in first and each st across, turn. In last st of row 12, sc color change to black. *(18 sc)*

Rows 13 & 14: Ch 1, sc in first and each st across, turn. In last st of row 14, sc color change to pumpkin. *(18 sc)*

Fasten off black.

Rows 15–18: Ch 1, sc in first and each st across, turn. *(18 sc)*

Fasten off, leaving a long tail for sewing.

BODY ASSEMBLY

See Basic Cube Body Assembly on page 2, joining in the following order: Beg by sewing 1 Solid Square *(bottom)* to pumpkin-only edge of 1 Striped Square *(side)*, sew rem 2 Striped Squares *(top and 2nd side)* with all seams made on a pumpkin-only edge to complete box shape. Sew rem 2 Solid Squares on open sides *(front and back)*.

MUZZLE

Rnd 1: With snow white, ch 2, 9 sc in 2nd ch from hook, **place stitch marker in first st, do not join** *(see Pattern Notes)*. *(9 sc)*

Rnd 2: 2 sc in each st around. *(18 sc)*

Rnd 3: [Sc in next st, 2 sc in next st] around. *(27 sc)*

Rnds 4–6: Sc in each st around. At end of rnd 6, **join** *(see Pattern Notes)* in first st. *(27 sc)*

Fasten off, leaving a 12-inch tail for sewing.

NOSE

With black, ch 2, 9 sc in 2nd ch from hook, join in first st. *(9 sts)*

Fasten off, leaving a 12-inch tail for sewing.

Sew completed Nose to center front of Muzzle over rnds 1–3 *(having nose sit slightly up from center)*.

With tail, embroider **straight stitches** *(see illustration)* to create a W shape directly below Nose, with center of W shape touching bottom of Nose.

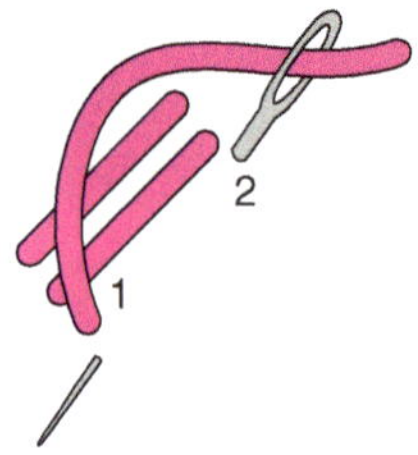

Straight Stitch

Sew finished Muzzle to center front of cube, leaving 3 rows under Muzzle and 6 rows above Muzzle.

EAR

Make 2.

Rnd 1: With snow white, ch 2, 9 sc in 2nd ch from hook, place stitch marker in first st, do not join. *(9 sc)*

Rnd 2: 2 sc in each st around. *(18 sc)*

Rnd 3: [Sc in next st, 2 sc in next st] around. *(27 sc)*

Rnd 4: Sc in each st to last st, sc color change to black in last st. *(27 sc)*

Fasten off white, leaving a 9-inch tail for sewing.

Fold circle in half with white tail and working yarn at beg of folded edge, working through both thicknesses, sc in each st along outer curved edge. *(13 sc)*

Fasten off.

With white tail, sew straight edge of Ears centered over top right and top left corners at front of cube.

TAIL

Rnd 1: With black, ch 2, 9 sc in 2nd ch from hook, place stitch marker in first st, do not join. *(9 sc)*

Rnd 2: [Sc in next 2 sts, 2 sc in next st] around, working sc color change to pumpkin in last st. *(12 sc)*

Rnd 3: Sc in each st around. *(12 sc)*

Rnds 4–6: Sc in each st around. In last st of rnd 6, sc color change to black. *(12 sc)*

Rnds 7–9: Sc in each st around. In last st of rnd 9, sc color change to pumpkin. *(12 sc)*

Rnds 10–13: Sc in each st around. In last st of rnd 13, sc color change to black. *(12 sc)*

Rnds 14–16: Sc in each st around. In last st of rnd 16, sc color change to pumpkin. *(12 sc)*

Fasten off black.

Rnds 17–20: Sc in each st around. At end of rnd 20, join in first st. *(12 sc)*

Fasten off, leaving a 9-inch tail for sewing.

Stuff and pinch end closed.

Sewing end of Tail closed while sewing to cube, sew to seam at center back base of cube.

LEG

Make 4.

Rnd 1: With snow white, ch 2, 9 sc in 2nd ch from hook, place stitch marker in first st, do not join. *(9 sc)*

Rnd 2: 2 sc in each st to last st, sc color change to pumpkin in last st. *(18 sc)*

Fasten off snow white.

Rnds 3 & 4: Sc in each st around. In last st of rnd 4, sc color change to black. *(18 sc)*

Rnds 5 & 6: Sc in each st around. In last st of rnd 6, sc color change to pumpkin. *(18 sc)*

Fasten off black.

Rnds 7 & 8: Sc in each st around. At end of rnd 8, join in first st. *(18 sc)*

Fasten off, leaving a 9-inch tail for sewing.

Lightly stuff and pinch end closed.

Sewing end of Legs closed while sewing to cube, sew 2 Legs to seam at base of center front, leaving roughly ½ inch between them. Sew back Legs in same manner to seam at base of sides, even with back of cube.

FINISHING

EYES

Sew a black button to center front of cube on each side of Muzzle with 5 rows above top of Eye.

Designer Tip

Add life to the Eyes by using acrylic paint to paint a thin line along the lower left edge of each button and adding 2 dots of paint in the upper right.

WHISKERS

Using photograph as a guide, with black and tapestry needle, embroider 3 straight stitches in an arrow shape on either side of Muzzle and below Eyes.

HENRY ROLLING PANDA

With its signature black and white color pattern, round ears and sweet little face, this crochet panda is sure to melt your heart.

SKILL LEVEL

Confident Beginner

FINISHED MEASUREMENT

Body is 5 inches square

MATERIALS

- Premier Yarns Anti-Pilling Everyday Worsted medium (worsted) weight acrylic yarn (3½ oz/180 yds/ 100g per skein):
  - 1 skein each #100-01 snow white and #100-12 black
- Size G/6/4mm crochet hook or size needed to obtain gauge
- Tapestry needle
- Stitch marker
- Polyester fiberfill
- ½-inch black buttons: 2*

**For use by children under 3 years of age, embroider eyes with black yarn.*

GAUGE

9 sc = 2 inches; 9 rows = 2 inches

Exact gauge is not critical for this project.

PATTERN NOTES

Each cubie is created by making 6 separate Squares flat and then sewing them together using whipstitches. Remaining pieces are worked separately and sewn on.

Leave a long tail for sewing on each remaining piece as specified. Weave in all other loose ends as work progresses unless otherwise stated.

Work remaining pieces in continuous rounds; do not join or turn unless otherwise stated. Place stitch marker at beginning of round and move up as each round is completed.

Join with a slip stitch unless otherwise stated.

Stuff firmly, but not so the stuffing shows through the stitches.

SPECIAL STITCH

Single crochet color change (sc color change): Insert hook in indicated st, yo, pull up a lp *(2 lps on hook)*, drop current color, yo with new color, draw through both lps *(see illustration)*. Cut color not in use unless otherwise stated.

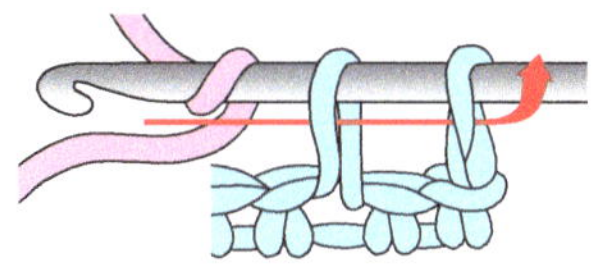

Single Crochet Color Change

PANDA

BASIC CUBE BODY

SOLID SQUARE

Make 3 in snow white.

See Basic Cube Body Square on page 2.

COLOR-BLOCK SQUARE

Make 3.

Row 1: With black, ch 19, sc in 2nd ch from hook and each rem ch across, turn. *(18 sc)*

Rows 2–9: Ch 1, sc in first and each st across, turn. In last st of row 9, **sc color change** *(see Special Stitch)* to snow white. *(18 sc)*

Rows 10–18: Ch 1, sc in first and each st across, turn. *(18 sc)*

Fasten off, leaving a long tail for sewing.

LEG

Make 4.

Rnd 1: With black, ch 2, 9 sc in 2nd ch from hook, **place stitch marker in first st, do not join** *(see Pattern Notes). (9 sc)*

Rnd 2: 2 sc in each st around. *(18 sc)*

Rnd 3: [Sc in next st, 2 sc in next st] around. *(27 sc)*

Rnds 4–10: Sc in each st around. At end of rnd 10, **join** *(see Pattern Notes)* in first st. *(27 sc)*

Fasten off, leaving a 9-inch tail for sewing.

Stuff and pinch ends closed.

Sewing end of Legs closed while sewing to cube, sew 2 Legs to seam at base of center front, leaving roughly ½ inch between them. Sew back Legs in same manner to seam at base of sides, even with back of cube.

BODY ASSEMBLY

See Basic Cube Body Assembly on page 2, joining in the following order: Beg by sewing 2 Color-Block Squares tog *(side and back)*, matching color along sides, sew last Color-Block Square in same orientation *(2nd side)*, sew 1 Solid Square *(front)* to end to complete box shape. With black, sew 1 Solid Square to mostly black opening *(top)* and with white, sew last Solid Square onto white opening *(bottom)*.

EAR

Make 2.

Rnd 1: With black, ch 2, 9 sc in 2nd ch from hook, place stitch marker in first st, do not join. *(9 sc)*

Rnd 2: 2 sc in each st around. *(18 sc)*

Rnds 3–6: Sc in each st around. *(18 sc)*

Fold circle in half with working yarn at beg of folded edge, working through both thicknesses, sc in each st along outer curved edge. *(9 sc)*

Fasten off, leaving a 9-inch tail for sewing.

With tail, sew straight edge of Ears behind seam at top front of cube, leaving 3 or 4 sts between them.

EYE CIRCLE

Make 2.

Rnd 1: With black, ch 2, 9 sc in 2nd ch from hook, place stitch marker in first st, do not join. *(9 sc)*

Rnd 2: 2 sc in each st around. *(18 sc)*

Rnd 3: [Sc in next st, 2 sc in next st] around. *(27 sts)*

Rnd 4: Sc in each st around, join in next st. *(27 sts)*

Fasten off, leaving a 12-inch tail for sewing.

Sew Eye Circles to front of cube, about 3 rows above front Legs and with 1 st between them.

MUZZLE

Rnd 1: With snow white, ch 2, 9 sc in 2nd ch from hook, place stitch marker in first st, do not join. *(9 sc)*

Rnd 2: 2 sc in each st around. *(18 sc)*

Rnd 3: [Sc in next st, 2 sc in next st] around. *(27 sc)*

Rnds 4–6: Sc in each st around. At end of rnd 6, join in next st.

Fasten off, leaving a 12-inch tail for sewing.

NOSE

Using photograph as a guide, with black, embroider **straight stitches** *(see illustration)* from center of Muzzle to sp between rnds 2 and 3, creating an inverted triangle shape and overlapping previous sts to create a solid Nose.

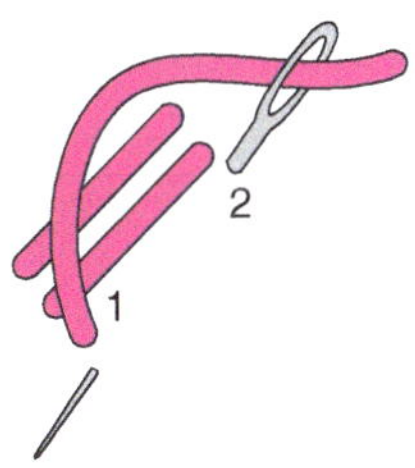

Straight Stitch

MOUTH

With black, embroider 2 straight stitches in an upside-down V shape with point of V originating at center of Muzzle directly under Nose.

Sew completed Muzzle to center front of cube, with 6 rows above and below and overlapping Eye Circles.

Stuff firmly just prior to closing.

FINISHING

EYES

Sew buttons to Eye Circles, making sure edge of buttons touch upper outer portion of Muzzle. ●

Designer Tip

Add life to the Eyes by using acrylic paint to paint a thin line along the lower left edge of each button and adding 2 dots of paint in the upper right.

KENZIE RESTING KOALA

The cuteness level is through the roof with this koala!
You won't be able to resist her charm.

SKILL LEVEL

Confident Beginner

FINISHED MEASUREMENT

Body is 5 inches square

MATERIALS

- Premier Yarns Anti-Pilling Everyday Worsted medium (worsted) weight acrylic yarn (3½ oz/180 yds/100g per skein):
  - 1 skein each #100-01 snow white, #100-12 black and #100-52 chinchilla
- Size G/6/4mm crochet hook or size needed to obtain gauge
- Tapestry needle
- Stitch marker
- Polyester fiberfill
- ½-inch black buttons: 2*

**For use by children under 3 years of age, embroider eyes with black yarn.*

GAUGE

9 sc = 2 inches; 9 rows = 2 inches

Exact gauge is not critical for this project.

PATTERN NOTES

Each cubie is created by making 6 separate Squares flat and then sewing them together using whipstitches. Remaining pieces are worked separately and sewn on.

Leave a long tail for sewing on each remaining piece as specified. Weave in all other loose ends as work progresses unless otherwise stated.

Work remaining pieces in continuous rounds; do not join or turn unless otherwise stated. Place stitch marker at beginning of round and move up as each round is completed.

Join with a slip stitch unless otherwise stated.

Stuff firmly, but not so the stuffing shows through the stitches.

SPECIAL STITCH

Single crochet color change (sc color change): Insert hook in indicated st, yo, pull up a lp *(2 lps on hook)*, drop current color, yo with new color, draw through both lps *(see illustration)*. Cut color not in use unless otherwise stated.

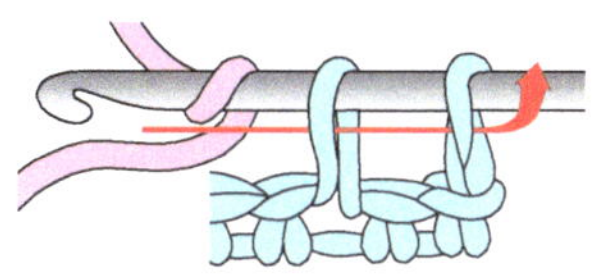

Single Crochet Color Change

KOALA

BASIC CUBE BODY

SOLID SQUARE

Make 5 with chinchilla and 1 with snow white.

See Basic Cube Body Square on page 2.

BODY ASSEMBLY

See Basic Cube Body Assembly on page 2 joining in the following order: Beg by sewing snow white Square *(bottom)* to 1 chinchilla Square *(side)*, sew rem 4 Squares as instructed in Basic Cube Body Assembly.

NOSE

Rnd 1: With black, ch 2, 9 sc in 2nd ch from hook, place stitch marker in first st, do not join. *(9 sc)*

Rnd 2: 2 sc in each st around. *(18 sc)*

Rnd 3: [Sc in next st, 2 sc in next st] around. *(27 sc)*

Rnds 4–6: Sc in each st around. At end of rnd 6, **join** *(see Pattern Notes)* in first st. *(27 sc)*

Fasten off, leaving a 12-inch tail for sewing.

Pinch sides slightly to create an oval shape. Keeping oval shape, sew to center front of cube with 4 rows above Nose and 4 sts on each side of Nose. Stuff firmly just prior to closing.

EAR

Make 2.

Rnd 1: With snow white, ch 2, 9 sc in 2nd ch from hook, **place stitch marker in first st, do not join** *(see Pattern Notes)*. *(9 sc)*

Rnd 2: 2 sc in each st around. *(18 sc)*

Rnd 3: [Sc in next st, 2 sc in next st] around. *(27 sc)*

Rnd 4: Sc in each st around. *(27 sc)*

Rnd 5: [Sc in next 2 sts, 2 sc in next st] around. *(36 sc)*

Rnd 6: Sc in each st to last st, **sc color change** *(see Special Stitch)* to chinchilla in last st. *(36 sc)*

Fasten off snow white.

Rnd 7: [Sc in next 3 sts, 2 sc in next st] around. *(45 sc)*

Rnd 8: Sc in each st around. *(45 sc)*

Fold circle in half with working yarn at beg of folded edge, working through both thicknesses, sc in each st along outer curved edge. *(22 sc)*

Fasten off, leaving a 9-inch tail.

With tail, sew straight edge of Ears along flat sides of cube front, with top of Ear curving over first inch along top of cube.

LEG

Make 4.

Rnd 1: With chinchilla, ch 2, 9 sc in 2nd ch from hook, place stitch marker in first st, do not join. *(9 sc)*

Rnd 2: 2 sc in each st around. *(18 sc)*

Rnd 3: [Sc in next st, 2 sc in next st] around. *(27 sc)*

Rnds 4–10: Sc in each st around. *(27 sc)*

Rnd 11: [Sc in next st, **sc dec** *(see Stitch Guide)* in next 2 sts] around. *(18 sc)*

Rnd 12: Sc in each st around, join in first st. *(18 sc)*

Fasten off, leaving a 9-inch tail for sewing.

Lightly stuff and pinch end closed.

Sewing end of Legs closed while sewing to cube, sew 2 Legs to seam at base of center front of cube, leaving roughly ½ inch between them. Sew back Legs in the same manner to seam at base of sides, even with back of cube.

FINISHING

EYES

Sew 2 black buttons to center front of cube even with top of nose and 1 st away on each side of Nose.

Designer Tip

Add life to the Eyes by using acrylic paint to paint a thin line along the lower left edge of each button and adding 2 dots of paint in the upper right.

LUNA NIGHT OWL

Make a whole parliament of owls, each with unique color combinations and differing placements of pupils.

SKILL LEVEL

Confident Beginner

FINISHED MEASUREMENT

Body is 5 inches square

MATERIALS

- Premier Yarns Anti-Pilling Everyday Worsted medium (worsted) weight acrylic yarn (3½ oz/180 yds/100g per skein):
  - 1 skein each #100-01 snow white, #100-14 caramel, #100-88 butter and #100-84 blueberry
  - Small amount #100-94 pumpkin
- Size G/6/4mm crochet hook or size needed to obtain gauge
- Tapestry needle
- Stitch marker
- Polyester fiberfill
- ½-inch black buttons: 2*

**For use by children under 3 years of age, embroider eyes with black yarn.*

GAUGE

9 sc = 2 inches; 9 rows = 2 inches

Exact gauge is not critical for this project.

PATTERN NOTES

Each cubie is created by making 6 separate Squares flat and then sewing them together using whipstitches. Remaining pieces are worked separately and sewn on.

Leave a long tail for sewing on each remaining piece as specified. Weave in all other loose ends as work progresses unless otherwise stated.

Work Eye and Wing in continuous rounds; do not join or turn unless otherwise stated.

Place stitch marker at beginning of round and move up as each round is completed.

When changing color on Striped Squares, carry unused color loosely up until next needed if not instructed to fasten off.

Join with a slip stitch unless otherwise stated.

Stuff firmly, but not so the stuffing shows through the stitches.

SPECIAL STITCH

Single crochet color change (sc color change): Insert hook in indicated st, yo, pull up a lp *(2 lps on hook)*, drop current color, yo with new color, draw through both lps *(see illustration)*.

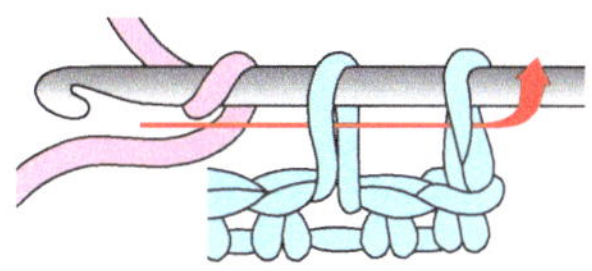

Single Crochet Color Change

BASIC CUBE BODY

SOLID SQUARE

Make 1 with butter and 1 with caramel.

See Basic Cube Body Square on page 2.

STRIPED SQUARE

Make 4.

Row 1: With butter, ch 19, sc in 2nd ch from hook and each rem ch across, turn. *(18 sc)*

Rows 2–10: Ch 1, sc in first and each st across, turn. In last st of row 10, **sc color change** *(see Special Stitch and Pattern Notes)* to blueberry. *(18 sc)*

Fasten off butter.

Rows 11 & 12: Ch 1, sc in first and each st across, turn. In last st of row 12, sc color change to caramel. *(18 sc)*

Rows 13 & 14: Ch 1, sc in first and each st across, turn. In last st of row 14, sc color change to blueberry. *(18 sc)*

Rows 15 & 16: Ch 1, sc in first and each st across, turn. In last st of row 16, sc color change to caramel. *(18 sc)*

Fasten off blueberry.

Rows 17 & 18: Ch 1, sc in first and each st across, turn. *(18 sc)*

Fasten off, leaving a long tail for sewing.

BODY ASSEMBLY

See Basic Cube Body Assembly on page 2, joining in the following order: Beg by sewing 2 Striped Squares tog *(front and side)*, matching stripes, sew rem 2 Striped Squares to previous Squares *(back and side)* matching stripes to create box shape. Sew butter Solid Square to butter edge of box shape *(top)* and caramel Solid Square on last open side *(bottom)* to finish cube.

EYE

Make 2.

Rnd 1: With snow white, ch 2, 9 sc in 2nd ch from hook, **place stitch marker in first st, do not join** *(see Pattern Notes). (9 sc)*

Rnd 2: 2 sc in each st around. *(18 sc)*

Rnd 3: [Sc in next st, 2 sc in next st] around, in last st, sc color change to blueberry. Fasten off snow white. *(27 sc)*

Rnd 4: Sc in each st around, **join** *(see Pattern Notes)* in first st. *(27 sc)*

Fasten off, leaving a 12-inch tail for sewing.

Sew buttons to Eyes at rnd 2 *(near edge, to make owl somewhat cross-eyed).*

Designer Tip

Add life to the Eyes by using acrylic paint to paint a thin line along the lower left edge of each button and adding 2 dots of paint in the upper right.

Sew finished Eyes to front of cube above stripes.

WING

Make 2.

Rnd 1: With caramel, ch 2, 9 sc in 2nd ch from hook, place stitch marker in first st, do not join. *(9 sc)*

Rnd 2: 2 sc in each st around. *(18 sc)*

Rnd 3: [Sc in next st, 2 sc in next st] around. *(27 sc)*

Rnd 4: Sc in each st around to last st, in last st, sc color change to blueberry. *(27 sc)*

Fasten off caramel.

Rnd 5: [Sc in next 2 sts, 2 sc in next st] around. *(36 sts)*

Fold circle in half with working yarn at beg of folded edge, working through both thicknesses, sc in each st along outer curved edge. *(18 sc)*

Fasten off, leaving a 9-inch tail for sewing.

Using photograph as a guide, sew finished Wings to top stripe on cube sides, oriented toward front of cube with curved edge facing down.

FINISHING

EARS

Hold 2 5-inch lengths of caramel and 2 5-inch lengths of blueberry tog. Tie 4-length bundle to top corner of cube front. Rep on other corner. Trim ends to 1 inch.

BEAK

With pumpkin and tapestry needle, embroider 4 or 5 vertical **straight stitches** *(see illustration)*, one on top of the other, between Eyes. ●

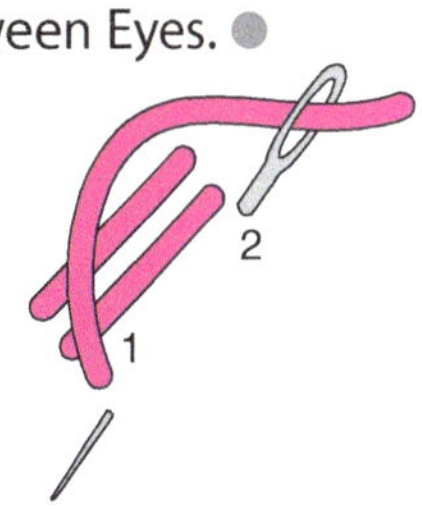

Straight Stitch

PETRO BLUE BUNNY

This bunny has his own unique charm that makes him perfect as a gift, home decor or even a collectible.

SKILL LEVEL

Confident Beginner

FINISHED MEASUREMENT

Body is 5 inches square

MATERIALS

- Premier Yarns Anti-Pilling Everyday Worsted medium (worsted) weight acrylic yarn (3½ oz/180 yds/ 100g per skein):
  - 1 skein each #100-01 snow white and #100-81 porcelain blue
  - Small amount #100-06 baby pink
- Size G/6/4mm crochet hook or size needed to obtain gauge
- Tapestry needle
- Stitch marker
- Polyester fiberfill
- ½-inch black buttons: 2*

**For use by children under 3 years of age, embroider eyes with black yarn.*

GAUGE

4½ sc = 1 inch; 4 rows = 1 inch

Exact gauge is not critical for this project.

PATTERN NOTES

Each cubie is created by making 6 separate Squares flat and then sewing them together using whipstitches. Remaining pieces are worked separately and sewn on.

Leave a long tail for sewing on each remaining piece as specified. Weave in all other loose ends as work progresses unless otherwise stated.

Work remaining pieces in continuous rounds; do not join or turn unless otherwise stated. Place stitch marker at beginning of round and move up as each round is completed.

Join with a slip stitch unless otherwise stated.

Stuff firmly, but not so the stuffing shows through the stitches.

SPECIAL STITCH

Single crochet color change (sc color change): Insert hook in indicated st, yo, pull up a lp *(2 lps on hook)*, drop current color, yo with new color, draw through both lps *(see illustration)*. Cut color not in use unless otherwise stated.

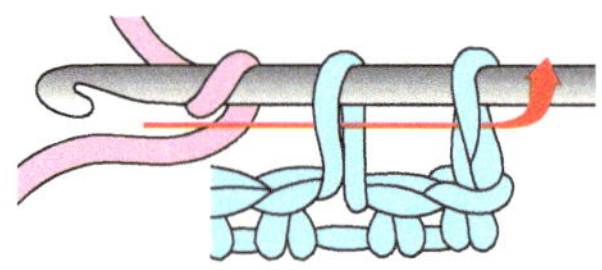

Single Crochet Color Change

BUNNY

BASIC CUBE BODY

SOLID SQUARE

Make 1 with snow white and 1 with porcelain blue.

See Basic Cube Body Square on page 2.

COLOR-BLOCKED SQUARE

Make 4.

Row 1: With snow white, ch 19, sc in 2nd ch from hook and each rem ch across, turn. *(18 sc)*

Rows 2–9: Ch 1, sc in each st across, turn. In last st of row 9, **sc color change** *(see Special Stitch)* to porcelain blue. *(18 sc)*

Rows 10–18: Ch 1, sc in each st across, turn. *(18 sc)*

Fasten off.

Rnd 8: Sc in each st around. *(18 sc)*

Rnd 9: [Sc in next 5 sts, 2 sc in next st] around. *(21 sc)*

Rnd 10: Sc in each st around. *(21 sc)*

Rnd 11: [Sc in next 6 sts, 2 sc in next st] around. *(24 sc)*

Rnd 12: Sc in each st around. *(24 sc)*

Rnd 13: [Sc in next 7 sts, 2 sc in next st] around. *(27 sc)*

Rnds 14–18: Sc in each st around. At end of rnd 18, **join** *(see Pattern Notes)* in first st. *(27 sc)*

Fasten off, leaving a **9-inch tail for sewing** *(see Pattern Notes).*

Fold last row in half. Working through both thicknesses of Ear, sew to top of cube toward front outer edge and with open edge of fold oriented toward front of cube.

Sew Ears tog with 1 or 2 small sts at roughly row 7 to keep Ears vertical.

CHEEK

Make 2.

Rnd 1: With snow white, ch 2, 9 sc in 2nd ch from hook, place stitch marker in first st. *(9 sc)*

BODY ASSEMBLY

See Basic Cube Body Assembly on page 2, joining in the following order: Beg by sewing 4 Color-Blocked Squares side by side and matching colors, then sew first and last Squares tog to form box shape *(front, back and sides)*. Orient box with porcelain blue at top and snow white at bottom. Sew porcelain blue Solid Square to top of box. Sew snow white Solid Square to bottom of box.

EAR

Make 2.

Rnd 1: With porcelain blue, ch 2, 6 sc in 2nd ch from hook, **place stitch marker in first st** *(see Pattern Notes). (6 sc)*

Rnd 2: [Sc in next st, 2 sc in next st] around. *(9 sc)*

Rnd 3: [Sc in next 2 sts, 2 sc in next st] around. *(12 sc)*

Rnd 4: Sc in each st around. *(12 sc)*

Rnd 5: [Sc in next 3 sts, 2 sc in next st] around. *(15 sc)*

Rnd 6: Sc in each st around. *(15 sc)*

Rnd 7: [Sc in next 4 sts, 2 sc in next st] around. *(18 sc)*

Rnd 2: 2 sc in each st around. *(18 sc)*

Rnd 3: [Sc in next st, 2 sc in next st] around. *(27 sc)*

Rnd 4: Sc in each st around, join in first st. *(27 sc)*

Fasten off, leaving a 12-inch tail for sewing.

Sew Cheeks to center front of cube, centered along color change line, making sure Cheeks touch in middle.

LEG

Make 4.

Rnd 1: With porcelain blue, ch 2, 9 sc in 2nd ch from hook, place stitch marker in first st. *(9 sc)*

Rnd 2: 2 sc in each st around. *(18 sc)*

Rnd 3: [Sc in next st, 2 sc in next st] around. *(27 sc)*

Rnds 4 & 5: Sc in each st around. In last sc of rnd 5, sc color change to snow white. *(27 sc)*

Rnds 6–10: Sc in each st around. *(27 sc)*

Rnd 11: [Sc in next st, **sc dec** *(see Stitch Guide)* in next 2 sts] around. *(18 sc)*

Rnd 12: Sc in each st around, join in first st. *(18 sc)*

Fasten off, leaving a 9-inch tail for sewing.

Stuff *(see Pattern Notes)* and pinch end of Leg closed.

Sewing end of all Legs closed while sewing to cube, sew 2 front Legs to center front of cube at base, leaving ½ inch between Legs. Sew back Legs in same manner to base of sides, oriented toward back.

TAIL

Rnd 1: With snow white, ch 2, 9 sc in 2nd ch from hook, place stitch marker in first st. *(9 sc)*

Rnd 2: 2 sc in each st around. *(18 sc)*

Rnds 3–6: Sc in each st around. *(18 sc)*

Rnd 7: [Sc dec in next 2 sts] around. *(9 sc)*

Fasten off, leaving a long tail for sewing.

Sew Tail to center back of cube at base, stuffing just prior to closing.

FINISHING

NOSE

With baby pink and tapestry needle, sew **straight stitches** *(see illustration)*, one on top of other, between Cheeks, just above where Cheeks meet.

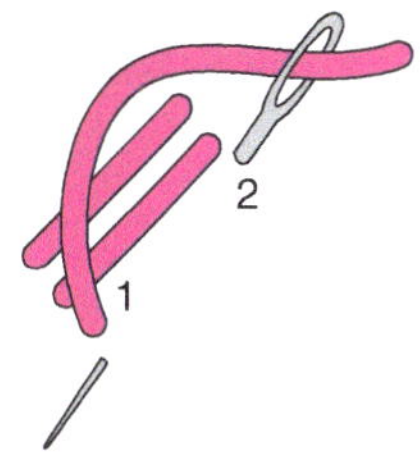

Straight Stitch

EYES

Sew buttons to center front of cube at row 15, leaving roughly 7 sts between Eyes.

Designer Tip

Add life to the Eyes by using acrylic paint to paint a thin line along the lower left edge of each button and adding 2 dots of paint in the upper right.

CORY SPUNKY CORGI

For those who love dogs, especially this precocious little breed, we offer this playful cubie.

SKILL LEVEL

Confident Beginner

FINISHED MEASUREMENT

Body is 5 inches square

MATERIALS

- Premier Yarns Anti-Pilling Everyday Worsted medium (worsted) weight acrylic yarn (3½ oz/180 yds/ 100g per skein):
  - 1 skein each #100-01 snow white and #100-14 caramel
  - Small amount #100-12 black
- Size G/6/4mm crochet hook or size needed to obtain gauge
- Tapestry needle
- Stitch marker
- Polyester fiberfill
- ½-inch black buttons: 2*

**For use by children under 3 years of age, embroider eyes with black yarn.*

GAUGE

4½ sc = 1 inch; 4 rows = 1 inch

Exact gauge is not critical for this project.

PATTERN NOTES

Each cubie is created by making 6 separate Squares flat and then sewing them together using whipstitches. Remaining pieces are worked separately and sewn on.

Leave a long tail for sewing on each remaining piece as specified. Weave in all other loose ends as work progresses unless otherwise stated.

Work remaining pieces in continuous rounds; do not join or turn unless otherwise stated. Place stitch marker at beginning of round and move up as each round is completed.

Join with a slip stitch unless otherwise stated.

Stuff firmly, but not so the stuffing shows through the stitches.

SPECIAL STITCH

Single crochet color change (sc color change): Insert hook in indicated st, yo, pull up a lp *(2 lps on hook)*, drop current color, yo with new color, draw through both lps *(see illustration)*. Cut color not in use unless otherwise stated.

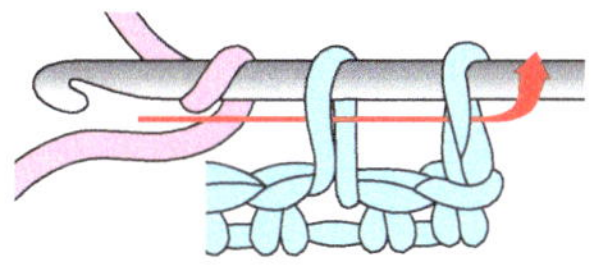

Single Crochet Color Change

CORGI

BASIC CUBE BODY

SOLID SQUARE

Make 3 with caramel and 1 with snow white.

See Basic Cube Body Square on page 2.

COLOR-BLOCKED SQUARE

Make 2.

Row 1: With snow white, ch 19, sc in 2nd ch from hook and each rem ch across, turn. *(18 sc)*

Rows 2–8: Ch 1, sc in each st across, turn. In last st of row 9, **sc color change** *(see Special Stitch)* to caramel. Fasten off snow white. *(18 sc)*

Rows 9–18: Ch 1, sc in each st across, turn. *(18 sc)*

Fasten off, leaving a long tail for sewing.

BODY ASSEMBLY

See Basic Cube Body Assembly on page 2, joining in the following order: Beg by sewing 4 Squares tog side by side starting with 1 Color-Blocked Square *(front)*, then 1 caramel Solid Square *(side)*, then 1 Color-Blocked Square *(back)*, then 1 caramel Square *(side)*. Sew first and last Squares tog to form box shape. Orient box with caramel at top and snow white at bottom. Sew rem caramel Solid Square to top of box. Sew snow white Solid Square to bottom of box.

MOUTH

Sew vertical straight stitch from bottom point of Nose going down approximately 1½ inches along center line of Muzzle.

Sew a ½-inch straight horizontal stitch at each side of bottom point of vertical stitch to create an upside down "T" shape.

Sew finished Muzzle to center front of cube between rows 6 and 12, **stuffing** *(see Pattern Notes)* just prior to closing.

MUZZLE

Rnd 1: With snow white, ch 2, 9 sc in 2nd ch from hook, **place stitch marker in first st** *(see Pattern Notes). (9 sc)*

Rnd 2: 2 sc in each st around. *(18 sc)*

Rnd 3: [Sc in next st, 2 sc in next st] around. *(27 sc)*

Rnds 4–6: Sc in each st around. At end of rnd 6, **join** *(see Pattern Notes)* in first st. Fasten off, leaving a **12-inch tail for sewing** *(see Pattern Notes).*

NOSE

With black, sew several **straight stitches** *(see illustration)*, from center of muzzle to between rnds 2 and 3. Place bottoms of straight stitches all in the same place, one on top of the other and tops of stitches side by side, creating a triangle shape. Make enough sts to shape Nose as desired.

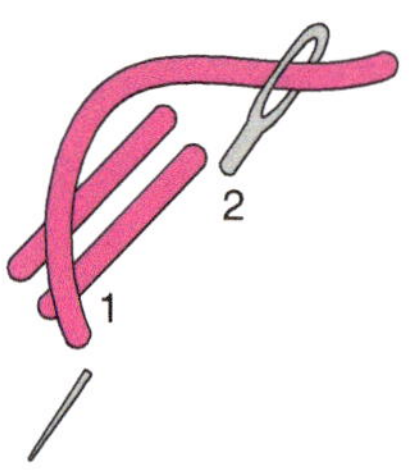

Straight Stitch

EAR

Make 2.

Rnd 1: With snow white, ch 2, 9 sc in 2nd ch from hook, place stitch marker in first st. *(9 sc)*

Rnd 2: 2 sc in each st around. *(18 sc)*

Rnd 3: [Sc in next st, 2 sc in next st] around, in last st, sc color change to caramel. Fasten off snow white. *(27 sc)*

Rnd 4: Sc in each st around. *(27 sc)*

Fold circle in half so that working yarn is at one side of folded edge. Working through both thicknesses, sc in each st along curved outer edge.

Fasten off, leaving a 9-inch tail for sewing.

Sew folded side of finished Ears to upper corners of front Square of cube.

Pinch top of each Ear to make Ear curve inward slightly, make a small stitch at pinched section to secure.

LEG

Make 4.

Rnd 1: With snow white, ch 2, 9 sc in 2nd ch from hook, place stitch marker in first st. *(9 sc)*

Rnd 2: 2 sc in each st around, in last st sc color change to caramel. *(18 sc)*

Rnds 3–10: Sc in each st around. At end of rnd 10, join in first st. Fasten off, leaving a 9-inch tail for sewing.

Stuff and pinch end of Leg closed.

Sewing end of all Legs closed while sewing to cube, sew 2 front Legs to center front of cube at base, leaving ½ inch between Legs. Sew back Legs in same manner to base of sides, oriented toward back.

TAIL

Rnd 1: With caramel, ch 2, 9 sc in 2nd ch from hook, place stitch marker in first st. *(9 sc)*

Rnd 2: [Sc in next 2 sts, 2 sc in next st] around. *(12 sc)*

Rnds 3–6: Sc in each st around. At end of rnd 6, join in first st. Fasten off, leaving a 9-inch tail for sewing.

Pinch end flat.

Sewing end of Tail closed while sewing to cube, sew Tail to center back of cube between rows 10 and 11.

FINISHING

EYES

Sew buttons to center front of cube on each side of Muzzle at roughly row 12.

Designer Tip

Add life to the Eyes by using acrylic paint to paint a thin line along the lower left edge of each button and adding 2 dots of paint in the upper right.

BETSY HIGHLAND COW

You will want to make a whole herd of these precious Highland cows in varying colors.

SKILL LEVEL

Confident Beginner

FINISHED MEASUREMENT

Body is 5 inches square

MATERIALS

- Premier Yarns Anti-Pilling Everyday Worsted medium (worsted) weight acrylic yarn (3½ oz/180 yds/ 100g per skein):
  - 1 skein each #100-61 rust, #100-88 butter and #100-12 black
- Size G/6/4mm crochet hook or size needed to obtain gauge
- Tapestry needle
- Stitch marker
- Polyester fiberfill
- ½-inch black buttons: 2*

**For use by children under 3 years of age, embroider eyes with black yarn.*

GAUGE

4½ sc = 1 inch; 4 rows = 1 inch

Exact gauge is not critical for this project.

PATTERN NOTES

Each cubie is created by making 6 separate Squares flat and then sewing them together using whipstitches. Remaining pieces are worked separately and sewn on.

Leave a long tail for sewing on each remaining piece, at whichever end of the piece will be attached to Body. If unsure which end will be attached, leave a long tail at both ends and weave in the unused tail later.

Weave in all other loose ends as work progresses unless otherwise stated.

Work Muzzle *(after row 6)* and Legs in continuous rounds; do not join or turn unless otherwise stated.

Place stitch marker at beginning of round and move up as each round is completed.

Join with a slip stitch unless otherwise stated.

Stuff firmly, but not so the stuffing shows through the stitches.

COW

BASIC CUBE BODY

SOLID SQUARE

Make 6 with rust.

See Basic Cube Body Square on page 2.

BODY ASSEMBLY

See Basic Cube Body Assembly on page 2, joining all 6 Squares to form Body.

MUZZLE

Row 1: With butter, ch 13, sc in 2nd ch from hook and each rem ch across, turn. *(12 sc)*

Rows 2–6: Ch 1, sc in each st across, turn.

***Note:** Beg working in rnds.*

Setup rnd (RS): Rotate to work in ends of rows, work 4 sc evenly sp across ends of rows, rotate to work in bottom of row 1, sc in each st across, rotate to work in ends of rows, work 4 sc evenly sp across ends of rows, rotate to work into sts of row 6, sc in each st across to beg of rnd, **place stitch marker in first st** *(see Pattern Notes). (32 sc)*

Rnds 1–3: Sc in each st around. At end of rnd 9, **join** *(see Pattern Notes)* in first st. Fasten off, **leaving a 12-inch tail for sewing** *(see Pattern Notes)*.

NOSTRILS

With black and tapestry needle, sew 1 vertical **straight stitch** *(see illustration)* for each nostril *(2 total)* over rows 4–6, leaving 8 sts between Nostrils.

Sew finished Muzzle to center front of cube between rows 3–12.

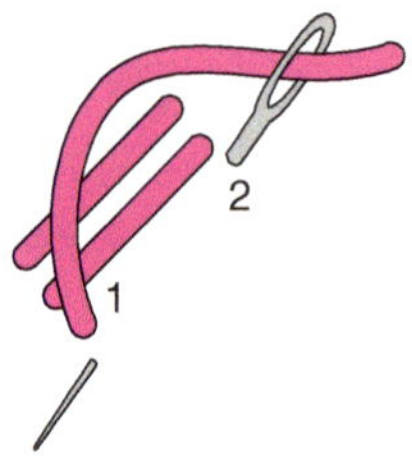

Straight Stitch

EAR

Make 2.

Rnd 1: With rust, ch 2, 6 sc in 2nd ch from hook, place stitch marker in first st. *(6 sc)*

Rnd 2: [Sc in next st, 2 sc in next st] around. *(9 sc)*

Rnd 3: [Sc in next 2 sts, 2 sc in next st] around. *(12 sc)*

Rnd 4: [Sc in next 3 sts, 2 sc in next st] around. *(15 sc)*

Rnd 5: [Sc in next 4 sts, 2 sc in next st] around. *(18 sc)*

Rnds 6–9: Sc in each st around. At end of rnd 9, join in first st. *(18 sc)*

Fasten off, leaving a 9-inch tail for sewing.

Fold piece in half and working through all thicknesses of Ear, sew to top side edge of cube, orientated toward front, with open side of folded Ear facing toward front.

HORN

Make 2.

Rnd 1: With butter, ch 2, 6 sc in 2nd ch from hook, place stitch marker in first st. *(6 sc)*

Rnd 2: [Sc in next st, 2 sc in next st] around. *(9 sc)*

Rnd 3: [Sc in next 2 sts, 2 sc in next st] around. *(12 sc)*

Rnds 4–9: Sc in each st around. At end of rnd 9, join in first st and fasten off, leaving a 9-inch tail for sewing.

Stuff *(see Pattern Notes)* Horn.

Sew finished Horns to top of cube between Ears, leaving roughly 1½ inches between Horns.

DOSSAN (BANGS)

Make 10.

Row 1: With rust, ch 201, sc in 2nd ch from hook and each rem ch across.

Fasten off, leaving a 12-inch tail for sewing.

Fold Dosan in half to form a loop. With tapestry needle and tail, sew Dosan randomly placed/oriented along top of cube in front of Ears and Horns.

LEG

Make 4.

Rnd 1: With black, ch 2, 6 sc in 2nd ch from hook, place stitch marker in first st. *(6 sc)*

Rnd 2: [Sc in next st, 2 sc in next st] around. *(9 sc)*

Rnd 3: [Sc in next 2 sts, 2 sc in next st] around, in last st **sc color change** *(see page 27)* to rust. Fasten off black. *(12 sc)*

Rnds 4–10: Sc in each st around. At end of rnd 10, join in first st.

Fasten off, leaving a 9-inch tail for sewing.

Stuff and pinch end of Leg closed.

Sewing end of all Legs closed while sewing to cube, sew 2 front Legs to center front of cube at base, leaving ½ inch between Legs. Sew back Legs in same manner to base of sides, oriented toward back.

TAIL

Row 1: With rust, ch 10, leaving an 8-inch tail for sewing, sc in 2nd ch from hook and each rem ch across, ch 1. *(9 sc)*

Fasten off.

Cut 12 4-inch lengths of rust and tie to last sc of row 1. Trim lengths to approximately 1½ inches.

Using long tail, sew completed Tail to center back of cube between rows 4 and 5.

FINISHING

EYES

Sew buttons to center front of cube at row 12 on each side of Muzzle, making sure Eyes touch side edges of Muzzle. ●

Designer Tip

Add life to the Eyes by using acrylic paint to paint a thin line along the lower left edge of each button and adding 2 dots of paint in the upper right.

HENRIETTA HAPPY CHICKEN

If you have a love of chickens, you can easily adapt the colors in this cubie to reflect your favorite breeds.

SKILL LEVEL

Confident Beginner

FINISHED MEASUREMENT

Body is 5 inches square

MATERIALS

- Premier Yarns Anti-Pilling Everyday Worsted medium (worsted) weight acrylic yarn (3½ oz/180 yds/ 100g per skein):
  - 1 skein each #100-01 snow white and #100-94 pumpkin
  - Small amount #100-07 really red and #100-28 mustard
- Size G/6/4mm crochet hook or size needed to obtain gauge
- Tapestry needle
- Stitch marker
- Polyester fiberfill
- ½-inch black buttons: 2*

4 MEDIUM

**For use by children under 3 years of age, embroider eyes with black yarn.*

GAUGE

4½ sc = 1 inch; 4 rows = 1 inch

Exact gauge is not critical for this project.

PATTERN NOTES

Each cubie is created by making 6 separate Squares flat and then sewing them together using whipstitches. Remaining pieces are worked separately and sewn on.

Leave a long tail for sewing on each remaining piece as specified. Weave in all other loose ends as work progresses unless otherwise stated.

Work Wings in continuous rounds; do not join or turn unless otherwise stated.

Place stitch marker at beginning of round and move up as each round is completed.

Stuff firmly, but not so the stuffing shows through the stitches.

CHICKEN

BASIC CUBE BODY

SOLID SQUARE

Make 1 with pumpkin and 5 with snow white.

See Basic Cube Body Square on page 2.

BODY ASSEMBLY

***Note:** The chicken is oriented on an angle, so the center of the face is a seam.*

See Basic Cube Body Assembly on page 2, joining in the following order: Beg by sewing 4 snow white Squares side by side, then sew first and last Squares tog to form box shape *(front, back and sides)*. Sew rem snow white Square to top of box. Sew pumpkin Square to bottom of box.

Rnd 3: [Sc in next st, 2 sc in next st] around. *(27 sc)*

Rnd 4: Sc in each st around. *(27 sc)*

Rnd 5: [Sc in next 2 sts, 2 sc in next st] around. *(36 sc)*

Rnd 6: Sc in each st around. *(36 sc)*

Fold circle in half so that working lp is at one side of fold. Working through both thicknesses, sc in each st along curved outer edge. Fasten off, leaving a 12-inch tail for sewing.

Orient cube so Comb is pointing toward front. Sew Wings to cube side on either side of comb, between rows 6 and 12, angling downward from center of Square toward back seam.

COMB

With really red, ch 10, [sl st in 2nd ch from hook, sc in next ch, 3 tr in next ch] 3 times *(3 bumps)*, ch 1, sl st in first ch, fasten off, leaving a **9-inch tail for sewing** *(see Pattern Notes)*.

Sew finished Comb to center of any corner of top of cube, oriented toward corner seam.

WING

Make 2.

Rnd 1: With snow white, ch 2, 9 sc in 2nd ch from hook, **place stitch marker in first st** *(see Pattern Notes)*. *(9 sc)*

Rnd 2: 2 sc in each st around. *(18 sc)*

FINISHING

BEAK

With mustard and tapestry needle, sew horizontal **straight stitches** *(see illustration)*, across front seam, beg approximately 1 inch below Comb. Beg with a 1-inch stitch for top of Beak, then make sts progressively smaller to bottom of Beak, placing sts one directly below another to form a triangle shape.

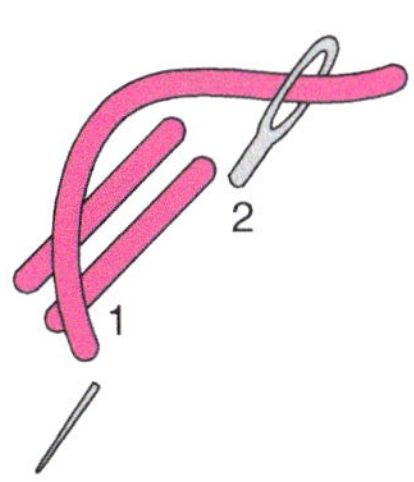

Straight Stitch

EYES

Sew black buttons to cube sides, on each side of and close to but not touching Beak, centered vertically at top st of Beak. ●

Designer Tip

Add life to the Eyes by using acrylic paint to paint a thin line along the lower left edge of each button and adding 2 dots of paint in the upper right.

PHINEAS LEAPING FROG

This cutie is sure to hop his way right into your heart, especially with that cockeyed grin.

SKILL LEVEL

Confident Beginner

FINISHED MEASUREMENT

Body is 5 inches square

MATERIALS

- Premier Yarns Anti-Pilling Everyday Worsted medium (worsted) weight acrylic yarn (3½ oz/180 yds/ 100g per skein):
  - 1 skein each #100-01 snow white, #100-16 kiwi and #100-28 mustard
  - Small amount #100-12 black
- Size G/6/4mm crochet hook or size needed to obtain gauge
- Tapestry needle
- Stitch marker
- Polyester fiberfill
- ½-inch black buttons: 2*

**For use by children under 3 years of age, embroider eyes with black yarn.*

GAUGE

4½ sc = 1 inch; 4 rows = 1 inch

Exact gauge is not critical for this project.

PATTERN NOTES

Each cubie is created by making 6 separate Squares flat and then sewing them together using whipstitches. Remaining pieces are worked separately and sewn on.

Leave a long tail for sewing on each remaining piece as specified. Weave in all other loose ends as work progresses unless otherwise stated.

When changing color on striped Legs/Arms, carry unused color loosely up until next needed, if not instructed to fasten off.

Work Eyes and Legs/Arms in continuous rounds; do not join or turn unless otherwise stated.

Place stitch marker at beginning of round and move up as each round is completed.

Join with a slip stitch unless otherwise stated.

Stuff firmly, but not so the stuffing shows through the stitches.

SPECIAL STITCH

Single crochet color change (sc color change): Insert hook in indicated st, yo, pull up a lp *(2 lps on hook)*, drop current color, yo with new color, draw through both lps *(see illustration)*.

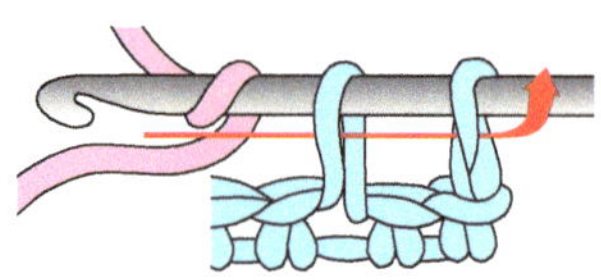

Single Crochet Color Change

FROG

BASIC CUBE BODY

SOLID SQUARE

Make 5 with kiwi and 1 with mustard.

See Basic Cube Body Square on page 2.

BODY ASSEMBLY

See Basic Cube Body Assembly on page 2, joining in the following order: Beg by sewing 4 kiwi Squares side by side, then sew first and last Squares tog to form box shape *(front, back and sides)*. Sew rem kiwi Square to top of box. Sew mustard Square to bottom of box.

EYE

Make 2.

Rnd 1: With snow white, ch 2, 9 sc in 2nd ch from hook, **place stitch marker in first st** *(see Pattern Notes)*. *(9 sc)*

Rnd 2: 2 sc in each st around. *(18 sc)*

Rnd 3: [Sc in next st, 2 sc in next st] around. *(27 sc)*

Rnds 4–6: Sc in each st around. In last st of rnd 6, **sc color change** *(see Special Stitch)* to kiwi. *(27 sc)*

Fasten off snow white.

Rnds 7–9: Sc in each st around. *(27 sc)*

Rnd 10: [Sc in next st, **sc dec** *(see Stitch Guide)* in next 2 sts] around. *(18 sc)*

Rnd 11: Sc in each st around. *(18 sc)*

Rnd 12: Sc dec in next 2 sts around, **join** *(see Pattern Notes)* in first st. *(9 sc)*

Fasten off, **leaving a 12-inch tail for sewing** *(see Pattern Notes)*.

With tapestry needle and working in **front lps** *(see Stitch Guide)* only, weave tail through all sts of last rnd, pull gently to close, weave in end to secure.

Orient Eye so kiwi section is at top and snow white section is at bottom.

Add black button to center front of each Eye so that top of button touches color change line.

Sew finished Eyes to top of cube, oriented toward front, so that Eyes touch in the middle.

Sew Eyes tog with a small stitch where they meet.

Designer Tip

Add life to the Eyes by using acrylic paint to paint a thin line along the lower left edge of each button and adding 2 dots of paint in the upper right.

LEG/ARM

Make 4.

Rnd 1: With kiwi, ch 2, 9 sc in 2nd ch from hook. Place stitch marker in first st. *(9 sc)*

Rnd 2: 2 sc in each st around. *(18 sc)*

Rnd 3: [Sc in next st, 2 sc in next st]. *(27 sc)*

Rnd 4: Sc in each st around. *(27 sc)*

Rnd 5: [Sc in next st, sc dec in next 2 sts] around. *(18 sc)*

Rnd 6: [Sc in next st, sc dec in next 2 sts] around. *(12 sc)*

Rnds 7–9: Sc in each st around. In last st of rnd 9, **sc color change** *(see Pattern Note)* to mustard. *(12 sc)*

Rnds 10–12: Sc in each st around. In last st of rnd 12, sc color change to kiwi. *(12 sc)*

Rnds 13–15: Sc in each st around. In last st of rnd 15, change color to mustard. *(12 sc)*

Rnds 16–18: Sc in each st around. In last st of rnd 18, change color to kiwi. *(12 sc)*

Fasten off mustard.

Rnds 19–21: Sc in each st around. At end of rnd 21, join in first st.

Fasten off, leaving a 9-inch tail for sewing.

Stuff rounded "bulb" end of Leg/Arm only and pinch top flat.

Sewing end of all Legs/Arms closed while sewing to cube, sew 2 Legs to front bottom seam of cube, at each side edge. Sew 2 Arms to top side seams of cube, one on each side and toward front corner.

FINISHING

MOUTH

With black and tapestry needle, sew 4 horizontal **straight stitches** *(see illustration)* between rows 12 and 13 of front, beg 2 sts left of center and making each st 2 sts long. This will form an off-center line ending about 3 sts away from seam.

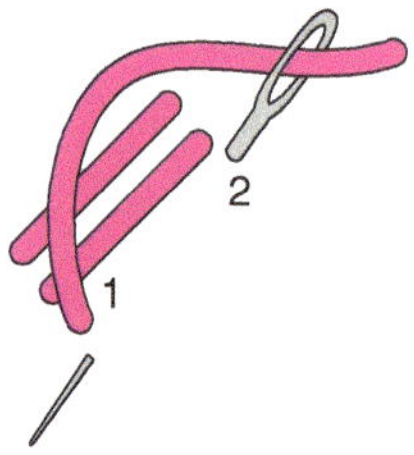

Straight Stitch

Sew 2 straight diagonal stitches, 1 st wide each, and angling up toward rows 14–16.

WILBER KING WHALE

Bring the ocean into your playroom or decor with this adorable little guy.

SKILL LEVEL
Confident Beginner

FINISHED MEASUREMENT
Body is 5 inches square

MATERIALS
- Premier Yarns Anti-Pilling Everyday Worsted medium (worsted) weight acrylic yarn (3½ oz/180 yds/ 100g per skein):
  - 1 skein each #100-81 porcelain blue and #100-84 blueberry
  - Small amount #100-01 snow white
- Size G/6/4mm crochet hook or size needed to obtain gauge
- Tapestry needle
- Stitch marker
- Polyester fiberfill
- ½-inch black buttons: 2*

**For use by children under 3 years of age, embroider eyes with black yarn.*

GAUGE
4½ sc = 1 inch; 4 rows = 1 inch

Exact gauge is not critical for this project.

PATTERN NOTES
Each cubie is created by making 6 separate Squares flat and then sewing them together using whipstitches. Remaining pieces are worked separately and sewn on.

Leave a long tail for sewing on each remaining piece as specified. Weave in all other loose ends as work progresses unless otherwise stated.

Work remaining pieces in continuous rounds; do not join or turn unless otherwise stated. Place stitch marker at beginning of round and move up as each round is completed.

Join with a slip stitch unless otherwise stated.

Stuff firmly, but not so the stuffing shows through the stitches.

SPECIAL STITCH
Single crochet color change (sc color change): Insert hook in indicated st, yo, pull up a lp *(2 lps on hook)*, drop current color, yo with new color, draw through both lps *(see illustration)*. Cut color not in use unless otherwise stated.

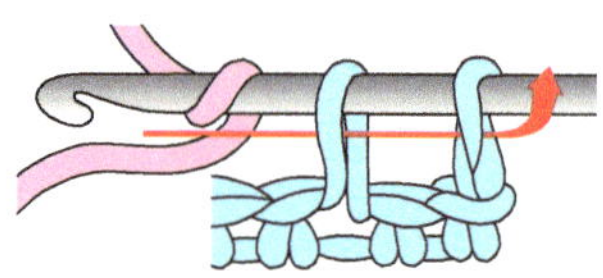

Single Crochet Color Change

WHALE

BASIC CUBE BODY

SOLID SQUARE
Make 1 with blueberry and 1 with porcelain blue.

See Basic Cube Body Square on page2.

COLOR-BLOCKED SQUARE
Make 4.

Row 1: With porcelain blue, ch 19, sc in 2nd ch from hook and each rem ch across, turn. *(18 sc)*

Rows 2–4: Ch 1, sc in first and each st across, turn. In last st of row 4, **sc color change** *(see Special Stitch)* to blueberry. Fasten off porcelain blue. *(18 sc)*

Rows 5–18: Ch 1, sc in each st across, turn. *(18 sc)*

Fasten off.

BODY ASSEMBLY

See Basic Cube Body Assembly on page 2, joining in the following order: Beg by sewing 4 Color-Blocked Squares side by side and matching colors, then sew first and last Squares tog to form box shape *(front, back and sides)*. Orient box with blueberry at top and porcelain blue at bottom. Sew blueberry Solid Square to top of box. Sew porcelain blue Solid Square to bottom of box.

FIN

Make 2.

Rnd 1: With porcelain blue, ch 2, 9 sc in 2nd ch from hook, **place stitch marker in first st** *(see Pattern Notes)*. *(9 sc)*

Rnd 2: 2 sc in each st around. *(18 sc)*

Rnd 3: [Sc in next st, 2 sc in next st] around. *(27 sc)*

Rnd 4: Sc in each st around. In last st of rnd, sc color change to blueberry. Fasten off porcelain blue. *(27 sc)*

Fold circle in half so that working yarn is at one end of fold. Working through both thicknesses, sc in each st along curved outer edge.

Fasten off, **leaving a 9-inch tail for sewing** *(see Pattern Notes)*.

Align straight edge of completed Fin with bottom seam on side of cube, close to back corner. Curved edge of Fin should be facing up.

Sew Fins to sides of cube over rows 1–4, along front half of curved edge of Fin.

TAIL

Make 2.

Rnd 1: With blueberry, ch 2, 9 sc in 2nd ch from hook, place stitch marker in first st. *(9 sc)*

Rnd 2: 2 sc in each st around. *(18 sc)*

Rnd 3: [Sc in next st, 2 sc in next st] around. *(27 sc)*

Rnd 4: Sc in each st around.

Fold circle in half so that working yarn is at one end of fold. Working through both thicknesses, sc in each st along curved outer edge.

Fasten off, leaving a 9-inch tail for sewing.

Hold both finished Tail pieces side by side with curved edges tog and matching ending corners where long tail for sewing is.

Using one long tail, sew Tail pieces tog starting at ending corner and across half curved edge.

Using other long tail, sew finished Tail to center bottom of back Square of cube, along row 5.

Attention Layout artist: insert top view photo here.

FINISHING

BLOWHOLE

With snow white, sew 2 **straight stitches** *(see illustration)* to form an "X" shape on center top of cube, over 5th and 6th rows from front edge.

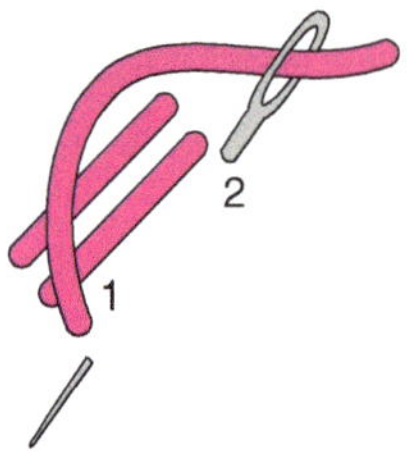

Straight Stitch

EYES

Sew buttons to front of cube along color change line and 2 or 3 sts in from each side edge. ●

Designer Tip

Add life to the Eyes by using acrylic paint to paint a thin line along the lower left edge of each button and adding 2 dots of paint in the upper right.

STITCH GUIDE

Need help? ▶ StitchGuide.com • ILLUSTRATED GUIDES • HOW-TO VIDEOS

STITCH ABBREVIATIONS

beg	begin/begins/beginning
bpdc	back post double crochet
bpsc	back post single crochet
bptr	back post treble crochet
CC	contrasting color
ch(s)	chain(s)
ch-	refers to chain or space previously made (i.e., ch-1 space)
ch sp(s)	chain space(s)
cl(s)	cluster(s)
cm	centimeter(s)
dc	double crochet (singular/plural)
dc dec	double crochet 2 or more stitches together, as indicated
dec	decrease/decreases/decreasing
dtr	double treble crochet
ext	extended
fpdc	front post double crochet
fpsc	front post single crochet
fptr	front post treble crochet
g	gram(s)
hdc	half double crochet
hdc dec	half double crochet 2 or more stitches together, as indicated
inc	increase/increases/increasing
lp(s)	loop(s)
MC	main color
mm	millimeter(s)
oz	ounce(s)
pc	popcorn(s)
rem	remain/remains/remaining
rep(s)	repeat(s)
rnd(s)	round(s)
RS	right side(s)
sc	single crochet (singular/plural)
sc dec	single crochet 2 or more stitches together, as indicated
sk	skip/skipped/skipping
sl st(s)	slip stitch(es)
sp(s)	space(s)/spaced
st(s)	stitch(es)
tog	together
tr	treble crochet
trtr	triple treble
WS	wrong side(s)
yd(s)	yard(s)
yo	yarn over

YARN CONVERSION

OUNCES TO GRAMS		GRAMS TO OUNCES	
1	28.4	25	⅞
2	56.7	40	1⅔
3	85.0	50	1¾
4	113.4	100	3½

UNITED STATES		UNITED KINGDOM
sl st (slip stitch)	=	sc (single crochet)
sc (single crochet)	=	dc (double crochet)
hdc (half double crochet)	=	htr (half treble crochet)
dc (double crochet)	=	tr (treble crochet)
tr (treble crochet)	=	dtr (double treble crochet)
dtr (double treble crochet)	=	ttr (triple treble crochet)
skip	=	miss

Single crochet decrease (sc dec): (Insert hook, yo, draw lp through) in each of the sts indicated, yo, draw through all lps on hook.

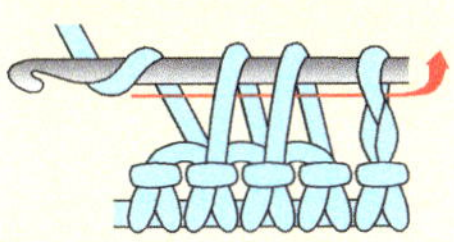

Example of 2-sc dec

Half double crochet decrease (hdc dec): (Yo, insert hook, yo, draw lp through) in each of the sts indicated, yo, draw through all lps on hook.

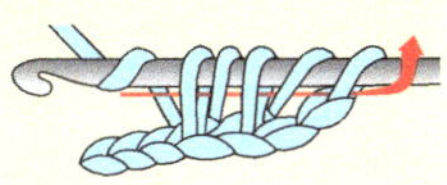

Example of 2-hdc dec

Reverse single crochet (reverse sc): Ch 1, sk first st, working from left to right, insert hook in next st from front to back, draw up lp on hook, yo and draw through both lps on hook.

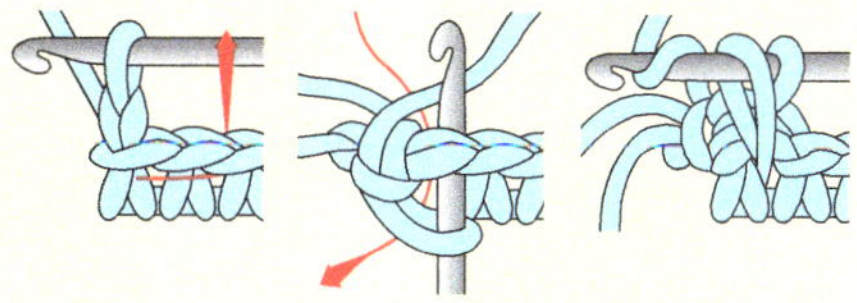

Chain (ch): Yo, pull through lp on hook.

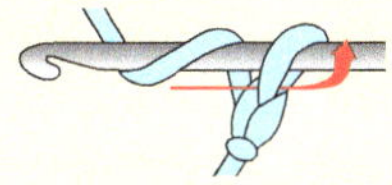

Single crochet (sc): Insert hook in st, yo, pull through st, yo, pull through both lps on hook.

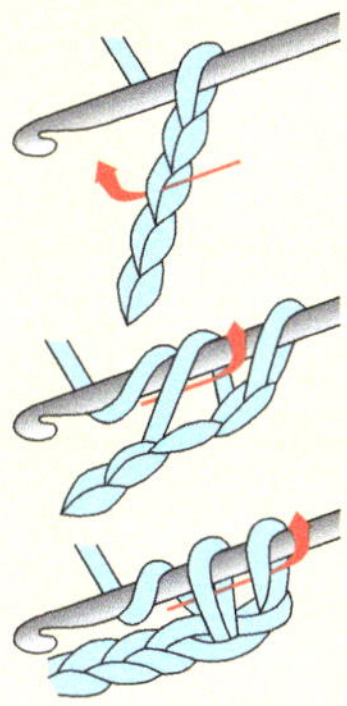

Double crochet (dc): Yo, insert hook in st, yo, pull through st, [yo, pull through 2 lps] twice.

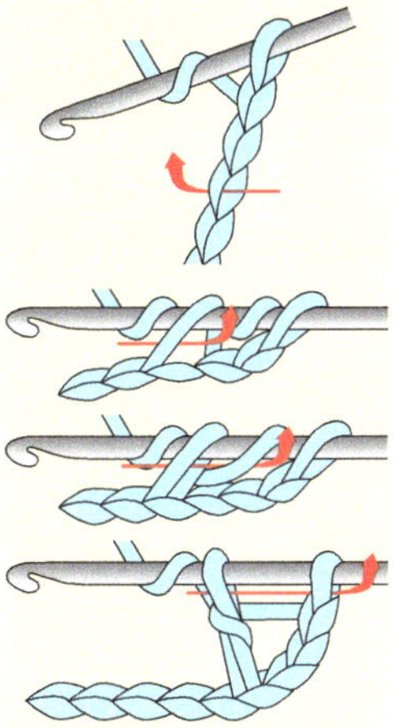

Double crochet decrease (dc dec): (Yo, insert hook, yo, draw lp through, yo, draw through 2 lps on hook) in each of the sts indicated, yo, draw through all lps on hook.

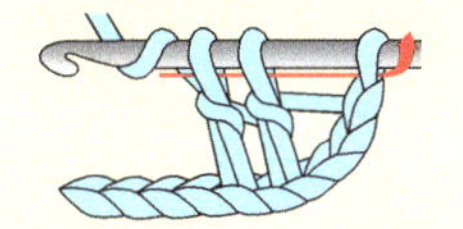

Example of 2-dc dec

Front loop (front lp):
Back loop (back lp):

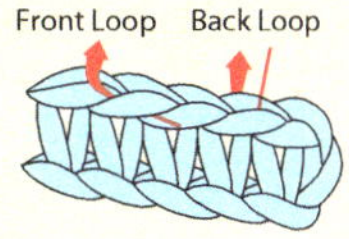

Front post stitch (fp):
Back post stitch (bp): When working post st, insert hook from right to left around post of st on previous row.

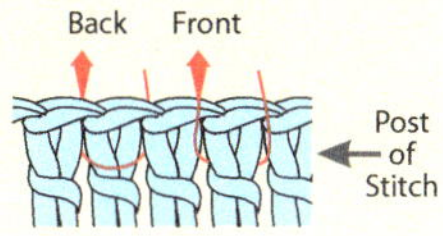

Half double crochet (hdc): Yo, insert hook in st, yo, pull through st, yo, pull through all 3 lps on hook.

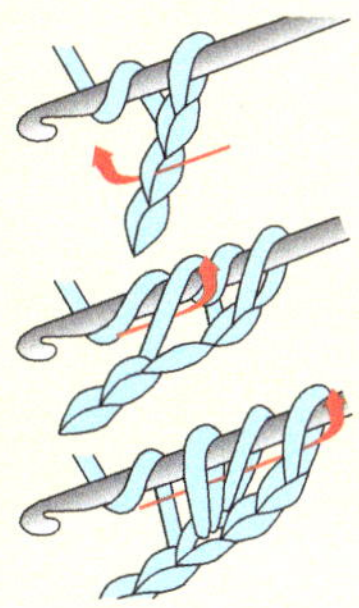

Double treble crochet (dtr): Yo 3 times, insert hook in st, yo, pull through st, [yo, pull through 2 lps] 4 times.

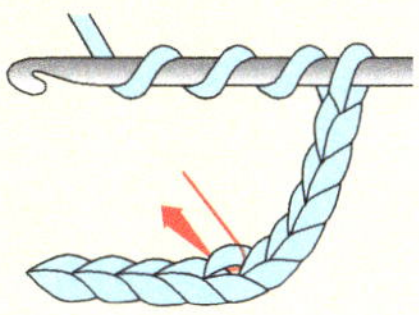

Treble crochet decrease (tr dec): Holding back last lp of each st, tr in each of the sts indicated, yo, pull through all lps on hook.

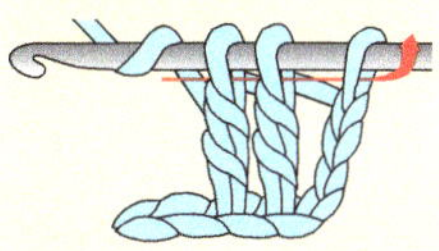

Example of 2-tr dec

Slip stitch (sl st): Insert hook in st, pull through both lps on hook.

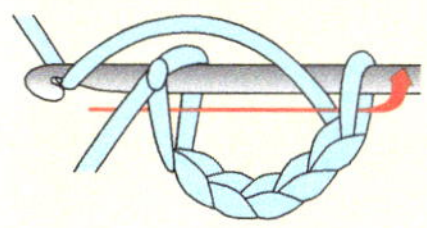

Chain color change (ch color change): Yo with new color, draw through last lp on hook.

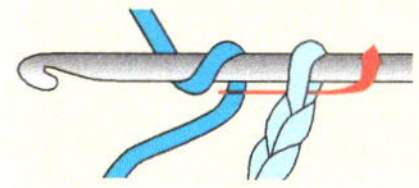

Double crochet color change (dc color change): Drop first color, yo with new color, draw through last 2 lps of st.

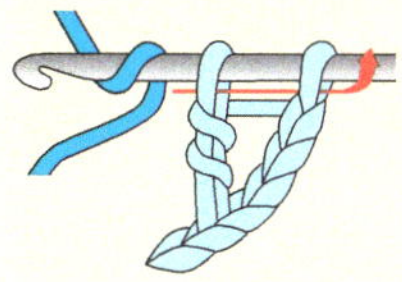

Treble crochet (tr): Yo twice, insert hook in st, yo, pull through st, [yo, pull through 2 lps] 3 times.

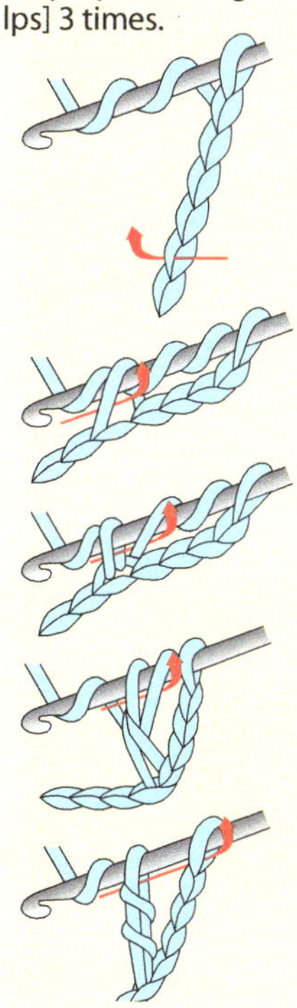

METRIC CONVERSION CHARTS

METRIC CONVERSIONS

yards	x	.9144	=	meters (m)
yards	x	91.44	=	centimeters (cm)
inches	x	2.54	=	centimeters (cm)
inches	x	25.40	=	millimeters (mm)
inches	x	.0254	=	meters (m)

centimeters	x	.3937	=	inches
meters	x	1.0936	=	yards

INCHES INTO MILLIMETERS & CENTIMETERS (Rounded off slightly)

inches	mm	cm	inches	cm	inches	cm	inches	cm
1/8	3	0.3	5	12.5	21	53.5	38	96.5
1/4	6	0.6	5 1/2	14	22	56	39	99
3/8	10	1	6	15	23	58.5	40	101.5
1/2	13	1.3	7	18	24	61	41	104
5/8	15	1.5	8	20.5	25	63.5	42	106.5
3/4	20	2	9	23	26	66	43	109
7/8	22	2.2	10	25.5	27	68.5	44	112
1	25	2.5	11	28	28	71	45	114.5
1 1/4	32	3.2	12	30.5	29	73.5	46	117
1 1/2	38	3.8	13	33	30	76	47	119.5
1 3/4	45	4.5	14	35.5	31	79	48	122
2	50	5	15	38	32	81.5	49	124.5
2 1/2	65	6.5	16	40.5	33	84	50	127
3	75	7.5	17	43	34	86.5		
3 1/2	90	9	18	46	35	89		
4	100	10	19	48.5	36	91.5		
4 1/2	115	11.5	20	51	37	94		

KNITTING NEEDLES CONVERSION CHART

Canada/U.S.	0	1	2	3	4	5	6	7	8	9	10	10½	11	13	15
Metric (mm)	2	2¼	2¾	3¼	3½	3¾	4	4½	5	5½	6	6½	8	9	10

CROCHET HOOKS CONVERSION CHART

Canada/U.S.	1/B	2/C	3/D	4/E	5/F	6/G	7	8/H	9/I	10/J	10½/K	N
Metric (mm)	2.25	2.75	3.25	3.5	3.75	4	4.5	5	5.5	6	6.5	9.0

Published by Annie's Attic, 306 E. Parr Road, Berne, IN 46711. Printed in USA.

ISBN: 979-8-89253-395-9
1 2 3 4 5 6 7 8 9